Buddhism: Beginner's Guide

Bring Peace and Happiness To Your Everyday Life

Positive Psychology Coaching Series®

D1016394

My Mailing list: If you would like to receive fresh info about **new Kindle reads** on social dynamics, psychology, career, NLP, success and healthy living for **free** <u>I invite you to my Mailing List.</u> Whenever my new book is out, I set the free period for two days. You will get an e-mail notification and will **be the first to get the book for $0.00** during its limited promotion.

Why would I do this when it took me countless hours to write these e-books?

First of all, that's my way of saying **"thank you"** to my new readers. Second of all – **I want to spread the word about my books and ideas.** Mind you that **I hate spam and e-mails that come too frequently** - no worries about that.

If you think that's a good idea and are in, just follow the link:

http://eepurl.com/R_UhP

Please be aware that every e-book and "short read" I publish is written truly by me, with thoroughly researched content 100% of the time. Unfortunately, **there's a huge number of low quality, cheaply outsourced spam titles on Kindle non-fiction market these days, created by various Internet marketing companies**. I don't tolerate these books. I want to provide you with high quality, so if you think that one of my books/short reads can be improved anyhow, please contact me at coachingpositivepsychology@gmail.com.

I will be very happy to hear from you, because that's who I write my books for.

Introduction

From one history of conflicts and wars to another story of freshly developing struggles and fights – this is the world we are living in. A world that is getting more and more chaotic as people get more educated, more modern, more informed, and so often more religious.

Middle East, Eastern Europe, South East Asia, and Africa are still freshly writing this script of wars and turmoil. Although the so-called developed world seems to be becoming more immune to civil strife such as internal and trans-border wars, it is becoming increasingly susceptible to family strife characterized by suicides, homicides and drug addictions.

Why is the magnitude of conflicts and wars increasing despite the education, advancing knowledge, sophisticated technology, big data stores, and more entrenched religion? It really seems paradoxical that despite all these advancements, we are getting more and more overwhelmed by our animalistic instincts towards destruction of ourselves and others. There must be critical ingredients lacking in our education, knowledge, technology, religions, and information, and whose lack of it is the cause of all these rising turmoil.

On my journey to run away from these evils and torments, I did find a torch of light in the far off rice fields of Thailand. It is this torch of light – Dharma, or simply the teachings of Buddha, that I endeavor to share with you in this book so that you too can liberate yourself from all forms of suffering.

"The pollution of the planet is only an outward reflection of an inner psychic pollution: millions of unconscious individuals not taking responsibility for their inner space." – Eckhart Tolle

Chapter 1: Why Buddhism?

On December 2007, I embarked on a mission to escape the boring winter and have a break from the shadows of my past. I chose to travel to Thailand... just to appreciate and learn more about the kind of rice that I always loved to cook that came from Southeast Asia. Exactly the kind of spontaneous and crazy backpacking trips I love.

One sunny day while I was walking down towards one of the rice fields, I saw a group of five people gathered down by a tree in what was plainly clear to me as monks with the simplest form of being – no hair, no shoes, loose robes, no chair or stool. They manifested a gentle mien and serene appearance and seemed unperturbed by the chaotic world around them.

They were very simple, taking on clean diet of boiled rice and some vegetables, using Thai sticks, which appeared as just a pair of thicker and more elongated toothpicks. No spoons, and still no plates as they were being served food on some kind of roundish basket on which a fitting piece of green banana leaf was spread under the food.

It was such a simplicity and big calm that baffled me. It created in me an inner desire to understand how they lived their lives in a way that manifested such a compelling authenticity of peace, harmony and serenity. I started seeking knowledge about their ways of life and started practicing the little things that I learned from them. Well, it did take me some time before I discovered that I was already in the middle of practicing Buddhism. What makes Buddhism so simple to start, yet so liberating? This is what I endeavor to uncover in this chapter and the rest that follow.

Buddhism Basics

Buddhism refers to the practice of teachings of Buddha. These teachings are many and diverse, as I will briefly highlight in Chapter 2. However, for purposes of a fast grasp of Buddhism, let's look at what Buddhism is not and what Buddhism is, in order to set ourselves on the right knowledge pedestal.

What Buddhism is Not;

- Is not a religion – Buddhism shares with major religions one common thing; doctrine. However, unlike others, it's not a religion per se. Though, still, there are those who have opted to refer to it or practice it as religion. What used to make me fear practicing Buddhism was my wrongly held belief that Buddhism was a weird and bizarre religion that was incompatible with Western ways of living. While in Thailand, under the tutelage of a Buddhist monk, I came to learn how Buddha encouraged his followers not to blindly follow, but arrive at their own truths about his teachings. This made me gain courage to explore more of his wisdom. No religion grants you this freedom to arrive at your own truths about it except Buddhism, which is simply 'a religion that is non-religious'. My increased awareness of Buddhism granted me the first step to pursuing my liberty by not rigidly holding onto any religion but exploring all religions as much as I can in search for truths without being ensnared by traps of dogmatism. Indeed, I was truly liberated.

- Is not ritualistic – Buddhism is not ritualistic. There could be certain rituals performed by adherents of Buddha, but they are merely cultural/traditional rather than doctrinal. Buddha teaches that you don't have to hold certain teachings, customs, practices, traditions, or beliefs as truths until you come to your own self realization of them as truths and practically useful to your life. Thus, I am a Buddhist who practices Buddhism in a non-ritualistic way. You are not stopped from following ritualistic practices as long as you don't become a slave of them. This granted me the second step of pursuing liberty. I stopped practicing all forms of religious rituals - I started sweeping away all forms ritualistic routines that I engaged in without knowing why I engage in them. Thus, I made a second step into attainment of my liberty. I felt myself becoming lighter, like a donkey whose heavy load had been relieved.

- Is not about deity – Buddhism, as a doctrine, and unlike religions, doesn't hold itself to any supreme or supernatural being. Rather, it is simply a teaching about good living. The greatest fear I had about Buddhism was that I had to turn away from my God in order to pursue other gods. This is one of the fears that my practice of Buddhism helped me get rid of. Indeed, I made a third step into attaining liberty. Not only have I gotten a clear understanding of Godliness, but I have also made greater strides in making myself purified.

- Is not about beliefs – Buddhism, unlike religions, is not held hostage to a founder's beliefs and neither does it hold people hostage to beliefs. Buddhism is about search for truth. If this truth goes against your held beliefs, so be it! Well, if this truth too goes against some or all of Buddha's teachings, that's OK as well! Buddhism liberates your conscience from the guilt of not following beliefs, be it new or ancient. I am now at liberty.

What Buddhism Is;

- Buddhism is spiritual – Buddhism is spiritual in the sense that it is non-religious and seeks truth in such a manner that helps you be the best being that you can be. Spirituality is about the essence of seeking your truest being.

- Buddhism is non-religious – the commonest tenets of religion are beliefs, rituals, deity and worship. However, Buddhism does not necessarily advocate for any of these except search for truth. Thus, Buddhism, unlike religions, does not bar you from attending to your religion but lets you seek truth in whatever religion you opt for. Every religion seeks truth as the highest aspiration and hence, in this regard, Buddhism is non-conflicting with religion.

- Buddhism is transcendental – because it's about truth, it goes beyond all boundaries of knowledge, religion, beliefs, superstitions, compartmentalization of life and all spheres and domains of life as we presume them. Hence, just as truth is, Buddhism is not limited by existing knowledge, it is not limited by culture, it is not limited by beliefs, it is not limited by traditions and it is not limited by one's religious persuasions.

- Buddhism is a way of life – Buddhism is not about an isolated element of your lifestyle. Buddhism is about the quality of every element of your lifestyle, be it relationship, career, academic pursuit, profession, religion, hopes, dreams, aspirations, etc.

What are the similarities between Buddhism and major religions?

The greatest similarity between Buddhism and all religions is that it has a doctrine. This doctrine is espoused by the teachings of Buddha. You can read more about these teachings in Chapter 2.

Why is Buddhism good for you?

Buddhism is good for you because:

- It allows you to overcome all obstacles that prevent you from seeking truth – Buddhism encourages you not to hold any position as truth unless and until you've discovered it. Thus, it discourages you from blindly holding onto beliefs, traditions and religions.

- It allows you to become enlightened – Buddhism insists that seeking truth is of supreme importance. And in seeking truth, so do you become enlightened. The main goal in Buddhism is to achieve Nirvana – a state that can be reached either during this earthly life or after death, according to practices like Tibetan Buddhism. It is a state of no suffering, no ignorance, and no wrong perceptions, but of great wisdom and calm, mastery of mind and amazing happiness.

- It boosts your health – Many researchers have concurred about the importance of Buddhism for your health. Through its practice of meditation and non-attachment to beliefs and traditions, you are able to confront your fears, control your emotions, discover truth, and thus avoid or overcome mental stress that can cause ravage to your mental and physical health. Before I knew anything about Buddhism and meditation, I was called a worrywart. I had hypertension problems, could not concentrate for longer than three minutes, my hands were shaking not only when I had to approach a girl, but also when I had to talk to my boss or to a plumber. I was a perfect example of underweight neurotic ectomorph. I calmed a little bit when I started traveling with my backpack, as that was a great form of meditation (and still is) - but the biggest shift in my life occurred when I started meditating everyday (which is a part of Buddhist practice) and totally changed my life philosophy according to the teachings of Buddha. Believe it or not, anyone who met me before my Buddhism journey wouldn't recognize me now at all.

- Buddhism enables you to understand your nature, the nature of beings, and the nature of things. This allows you to be at peace and live in harmony with every being and every thing. Helps you to be at peace, calm, awakened, and thus be able to live in the present without bitterness and regrets of the past or worries of the future.

- Buddhism helps you to discover, know, and understand your suffering. By this, you are able to live in reality without blaming and escapism.

- Buddhism advocates for full and genuine social transformation as emanating from one's being. The very reasons why political systems fail to effectively transform societies is because those who set up and run such systems have bad intent; greed, aggression, and delusion. Thus, for a political system to succeed in bringing about social transformation, it must be driven by loving-kindness, wisdom and generosity.

What is the essence of Buddhism?

The answer can be simple – the essence of Buddhism is joy, calm and wisdom. The joy that, according to these teachings, is always present in our minds, but not always accessible for us. The calm gives us the access to the unconditional joy that is not connected to any transient and passing events in our lives, which makes our happiness transcendent. It also gives us many other abilities, such as the ability to love a person not because of their attractiveness, niceness, or compliance with our standards, but just because of their very existence, which in turn enables us to fill our social relations with compassion and calmness.

Buddha once said that "after his time" there will be many new religions emerging, and most of them will be good, but none of them will be more important than human happiness.

"This is my simple religion. There is no need for temples; no need for complicated philosophy. Our own brain, our own heart is our temple; the philosophy is kindness. Whether one believes in a religion or not, and whether one believes in rebirth or not, there isn't anyone who doesn't appreciate kindness and compassion." - Dalai Lama

Should we perceive Buddhism as a coherent belief system?

Just like any other philosophical beliefs and religions, Buddhism also has its different branches. While Christianity in general consists of Catholics and Protestants, which include Baptists, Lutherans, Methodists and many other factions, and most Muslims are of Sunni or Shia denominations etc. - Buddhism contains three main Schools of Thought. Although I don't think that this kind of knowledge is the most important when it comes to understand Buddhism, and you could easily grasp the basics of these wise teachings without even being able to tell one branch from another, let me briefly present them to you to avoid misunderstandings.

Three Branches of Buddhism:

- Theravada

- Mahayana (Including Pure Land, Nichiren, Zen Buddhism)

- Vajrayana

Each of these branches evolved around different times, places, and incorporated different cultural elements. Nevertheless:

- All hold the Buddha as teacher.

- All embrace the Four Noble Truths and The Noble Eightfold Path (although some feature these more important than others) about which you will read further in this book.

- All believe that enlightenment is accessible for everyone.

- All preach that Buddha-hood (a state of perfect enlightenment) is the highest acquirement.

So what are the differences between these Schools of Thought?

1. **Theravada** (translated as "Doctrine of the Elders"):

    - Formed around 100 BCE, most popular in Sri Lanka, Thailand, Myanmar, Laos, and Cambodia, Theravada claims to be the most equivalent to the original teachings of the Buddha. It has a collection of written sermons, rules and teachings. The most important texts of Theravada are **Pali Tipitaka** and **Jataka,** originally written in Pali language. Nowadays, about 124,000,000 people follow Theravadan teachings.

- **Theravada** holds that the highest virtue is wisdom.

- The ultimate goal is to enter Nirvana (Nibbana), a ceassation of suffering.

- As Theravada was my first form of contact with Buddhism, I will be referring mainly to this branch in this book. I hold that because of Theravada's simplicity and genuineness, it is the best point to start your journey with Buddhism.

2. **Mahayana** (Also known as "The Big Vehicle"):

- Prominent in China, Japan, Mongolia, Tibet, Vietnam, and Korea, the Mahayana formed around 100 CE and it is considered to have about 185,000,000 followers these days. **Mahayana** accepts the Theravada's canonical texts, but also includes many other philosophical and devotional writings.

- The highest virtue in Mahayana is compassion (or karuna).

- Mahayana believes in Bodhisattvas – enlightened beings who postpone their Nirvana and come back to this earthly life to help other people achieve their enlightenment.

- Mahayana also comes up with idea of many godly creatures, including Bodhisattvas, Buddhas, and other powerful beings (such as Avolokiteshvara, Manjushri, Amithabha or goddess Tara) and a big bundle of means of worship towards them – however, they can be slightly different in each country, depending on its cultural background and characteristics.

3. **Vajrayana** (also known as "Diamond" or "Thunderbolt Vehicle" and "Tantric Buddhism"):

- Dominant in Tibet and newest of the three major branches, Vajrayana appeared around 500 CE and is said to have about 6,000,000 followers.

- Vajrayana puts significance on roles of gurus and lamas – although it shares many notions of Mahayana, it is more ritually based than Theravada and Mahayana. The beliefs involve the rituals of mantra recitation, meditation practices, mandalas and visualizations.

- Vajrayana does not have a single narrative – instead, significant teachers or monks explain the doctrine – Tantras are believed to be too hard to understand without an experienced teacher.

Of course, there are countless other Buddhist sects, but knowing these three is definitely enough for a good start. What all of them have in common is that they are like a clear diamond – the color changes when put on a different cloth - so that some rituals or beliefs may vary depending on the country and culture, even within one School of Thought. I'm sure that, for instance, Theravada Buddhism is slightly different in the US, UK, Spain, and in Mongolia. But that's the beauty of it. It gracefully shows the characteristic of each culture, nation and language.

But who exactly was the Buddha and what were his teachings all about? Let's find out in the next chapter...

Chapter 2: Buddha's Life and Teachings

You cannot fully understand the source of Buddha's teachings without having a perspective of what formed them – the life of Buddha.

The Life of Buddha

Buddha was born of King Suddhodana and Queen Maya of the Kingdom of Kapilavastu (modern India) as Siddhartha around 566 BC. Soon after his birth, the wise men predicted that he would become a Buddha (the enlightened one) to the chagrin of his father, who wanted him to become a great and authoritative ruler. To prevent their prophecy from becoming true, the King lavished Siddhartha in three secluded palaces and provided him with everything he needed. Siddhartha lived in these lavish palaces with his wife, Yasodhara. When he was around twenty-nine years old, Siddhartha became completely disillusioned with the rich life and privileges which made him seek adventure outside the palace. The four trips he made manifested in him four critical things that transformed his life.

On his first three trips, he saw sickness, old age, and death – things that he had never witnessed while in the palace. This prompted him to ask "How can I enjoy a life of pleasure when there is so much suffering in the world?" In his fourth trip, he encountered a wandering monk who had given up everything he ever owned to seek and end suffering. Siddhartha became inspired and promised to be like the monk.

He left the palace and became a wandering monk and thus renounced his royal pleasures in search of truth about how to end suffering. He shaved himself, removed all his princely clothes, wore robes, and called himself **Gautama**.

Siddhartha started practicing severe asceticism (eating only roots, leaves, and fruits, and at times interspersed with fasting) for six years on the false notion that this would lead him achieving enlightenment. However, he realized that this path was taking him nowhere and found out that neither his life of asceticism nor of luxury in the palace gave him the way of enlightenment. Thus, he quit asceticism and started eating well.

On a full moon day, Buddha went to sit under Bodhi tree in deep meditations and declared unto himself, "I will not leave this spot until I find an end to suffering." He eventually came to the realization of the cause of suffering, and thus became 'Buddha' meaning the 'Awakened one'. Thenceforth, he became known as **Shakyamuni Buddha.**

The Teachings of Buddha

The teachings of Buddha are based on the following key principles as elaborated further in Chapter 3.

- The **Three Universal Truths** – the three universal truths are those key truths that forms the basis of our universe.

- The **Four Noble Truths** – These four noble truths are truths about suffering.

- The **Noble Eightfold Path** – These are the eight paths demonstrated by **Turning of the Dharma Wheel** by Buddha in his preaching.

- The **Five Precepts** – These are the basic rules (I call them 'Five Commandments') that guide those adherents of Buddha's teachings.

- The **Wheel of Life** – This holds that life is a continuous process and thus death is not the end of life.

Chapter 3: Basics of Buddhism – Buddha's Principles

The best way to understand Buddhism is to learn its basic principles. The principles are:

1. The Path of Inquiry

2. The Three Universal Truths

3. The Four Noble Truths

4. The Eightfold Paths

5. The Five Precepts

The Path of Inquiry

Buddha warned his followers not to hold onto faith and beliefs blindly. He encouraged them to follow the way of truthful inquiry through meditation, and challenged them to make informed examinations even on his own teachings. Siddhartha often warned against fashioning their beliefs based on traditions, hearsay, words of a supernatural being, authority of ancient scriptures, elders, priests, teachers, etc.

As taught by Buddha, when you are traveling on the path of inquiry, you must keep your mind open and bereft of any beliefs, traditions, and prejudices or unexplored knowledge in order to investigate your own experience of in the most tolerant way.

Thus, it is only by you exploring and discovering for yourself that your particular belief or tradition is valid and relevant to your experience, only then can such a belief and or tradition lead to your own happiness and that of others.

I experienced this very truth in my own life. When I got my first serious job in a HR department, I was really happy initially. That was one of my dreams at the time and I totally wanted to climb on the career ladders as high as I could to eventually become a HR manager and a renowned headhunter. But there was a problem and it had grew like a snowball rolling down an Alpine peak – I soon started feeling that something was very wrong. After few months, my good mood started to melt. I experienced that time is flowing faster and faster, so that I had huge problems with telling one day from another. Like in the Nine Inch Nails song – every day was exactly the same and I couldn't find a moment to stop and look where was I really going.

At the beginning I was quite sure that it might have been caused by the long and extremely cold winter, but that wasn't the case. I soon discovered that the problem was lying in my mind, but I wasn't sure what it was exactly. Then my motivation started to dilute. After half a year I started feeling really depressed and found it really hard to finish even the simplest tasks. It took me a little bit longer to realize what the real problem was. The truth was harsh – I've seen this happen before, but was never pushed enough to notice and admit it – I never really wanted a job. I didn't want to sit on LinkedIn, database, Excel, and job boards all day, while hanging on the phone and leading international conversations about which I couldn't care less. I never wanted to work in a supermarket or a bakery again neither. I wanted to be free, to be my own boss and to travel more often. I just lived in the delusion that this job would buy me prestige, earn me money, and allow me to lead happy life, but I sold almost all of my free time and good spirit instead and became miserable.

The problem was that I blindly believed the social/family/coworkers' narrative of how "proper job" and career would make me happy and rich. Everyone was constantly telling me how a good university degree and high position in a good company would make me feel fulfilled, and I blindly believed them, without deeply reflecting on my own values. I just wanted more free time so I could record my music, travel, swim, and read my books - even with lower salary as a consequence. I knew people who earned lots of money in their prestigious jobs and I was given the same chance, but I knew that it would make me even more depressed, skinny, nervous and unhappy. Because I could not leave the job immediately, I stayed there for some time, but promised myself that I would start my own business as soon as possible. And so I did, which was the best decision I've made so far. Since that happened, I'm committed to never listening to anybody when it comes to my own path and happiness. Henry Ford once said: "If I had asked people what they wanted, they would have said: faster horses." More than that, if given a chance I would have probably never lost massive money on a University degree and probably started my own business earlier. That was my family I believed and my friends' lives I tried to copy instead of going my way. Buddhism helped me to eventually see that and gave me courage to change my boring life. I started to trust myself.

"Believe nothing, no matter where you read it, or who said it, no matter if I have said it, unless it agrees with your own reason and your own common sense." - Gautama Buddha

The Three Universal Truths

The three universal truths are those truths that Buddha experienced when he sat under a tree and marveled at the beauty of the flora. While still marveling, he saw a farmer beat his ox and a bird pick an earthworm. These last two occurrences disturbed him a lot and it is upon meditating on them that he discovered the three universal truths:

1. Nothing is lost in the universe – this conforms to the scientific notion that matter can neither be created nor destroyed but can be changed from one form to another. That means that there's no such thing as death, which is a very relieving notion, on which I will expand on later in this book.

2. Everything changes – there is nothing static. Every moment every life situation is changing. This conforms to the modern notion that the only thing that doesn't change is change itself.

3. Every cause has an effect – this conforms to the notion that every action has a reaction and that "you reap what you sow", as I like to put it, which is a very practical teaching. In modern studies, we always look at cause-and-effect relationship to

discover the scientific facts, social and philosophical truths. In Buddhism, this cause-and-effect relationship is what is summed up as Karma.

The Four Noble Truths

The Four Noble truths are clearly depicted in one of the occurrences in Buddha's life. A woman by the name Kisagotami lost her first and beloved son. She could not accept the fact that her cherished child had died and thus kept carrying him on the streets seeking anyone with the knowledge and power to help her resuscitate him. In her desperate endeavor, she encountered a wise and kind man who took her to Buddha.

Buddha heard her case and call for help. He instructed her "Fetch me a handful of mustard seeds from a family that hasn't lost any relative to death and I will bring your child back to life." The woman eagerly went from house to house in the entire village knocking to get mustard seeds from a house which had no known lost relative. She couldn't find any.

She came back to Buddha and before Buddha could say anything, she confessed "There is death in every family. Everyone dies. Now I understand your teaching." Yes, the lady discovered truth on her own path. Buddha responded to her "No one can escape death and unhappiness. If people expect only happiness in life, they will be disappointed."

From this, Buddha came with **Four Noble Truths** to guide his followers;

1. There is suffering and **suffering is common to all**.

2. **We are the cause of our own suffering**.

3. **We can end suffering** by doing away with that which causes suffering.

4. **The path to end suffering is enlightenment** and everyone can be enlightened.

The Nature of Suffering

Suffering permeates all sectors of our lives. We experience the agony at birth, when we are sick, when we are fighting the fallibility of old age, and when we are experiencing death. Our existence is inevitably marked with these three characteristics: *Annica* – also known as impermanence, *Dukkha* – dissatisfaction and *Annata* – non-self.

Impermanence means that no form is eternal in this world. Forms are constantly changing from one to another. If there's an apple, you eat it and throw the core away – that particular apple is no more, but it doesn't mean it has vanished – the core will give life to new bacteria, fungus and plants, while the parts you ate will nourish your being and get into your cells. So that physical manifestations of things are impermanent, and yet continual.

Dissatisfaction means that if you want to find lasting fulfillment in either physical or even psychological sphere, you will end up disappointed.

I will tell you about "non-self" in the next paragraph.

What's important is that we may not stop suffering from occurring at all, but we may lessen it and change the way we experience it.

"Have compassion for all beings, rich and poor alike; each has their suffering. Some suffer too much, others too little."- Gautama Buddha

The Causes of Suffering

Buddha informs us that we live in a sea of suffering due to our own ignorance and selfish desires. We are ignorant of the inevitable law of Karma and are obsessively engrossed in pursuit of our desires to accomplish wrong kind of pleasures.

The selfish desires can be understood as the needs we want to fulfill when our ego is overgrown – these may include collecting too many material possessions, getting in debt just to put on the ritz and impressing others, getting in too many intimate relationships that result in hurting others, overeating, overly obsessing over looks and physical appearance, blaming others and elevating ourselves and countless other actions that result in multiplying our (and not only our) suffering.

Buddha also taught about "Three Poisons": ignorance, aversion, and attachment.

Let me now briefly explain what "ignorance" means in Buddhism – first of all, it can have exactly the same meaning as what it means according to "common sense" or by the definition in a dictionary, but more than that – it states that one is identifying oneself as detached from everything else. It is a false perception that there's "me" that is not a fraction of something unlimited, of the whole Universe. It's a belief that everything else is definitely not "me", but something different.

That in turn leads us to something called as "dualistic view", as there's "me", or "I", and "others". When the distinction is made, it causes two contrasting ways of attitude: either something is good, and we want it, or it is not good, and we don't crave for it, or maybe even are alarmed by it.

So now we have two disparate sides: there are things that we don't want, so they may be dangerous, ugly or unlucky for us – because of this approach aversion, hate and doubt arises.

Contrastingly, there are the things that are so good that we can't stop thinking about them, so we create attachment, jealousy, distraction, or obsession.

"Too much self-centered attitude, you see, brings isolation. Result: loneliness, fear, anger. The extreme self-centered attitude is the source of suffering." - Dalai Lama

The Responsibility to Ending Suffering

Your responsibility to ending suffering is to free yourself from all forms of ignorance and selfish desires. To achieve this you must engage yourself into the right view/perspective of reality so that you are able to engender a harmonious existence between your nature of being, the nature of other beings and the nature of things. By ending ignorance and selfish desires so do you get enlightened, and by getting enlightened so do you enter nirvana – a state of joy, peace, and harmony. You can end this ignorance by getting to understand and practice Dharma (Buddha's teachings or doctrine of Buddha).

The Path to Ending Suffering

In order to achieve these Four Noble Truths, you need to walk the way of truth. In this regard, Buddha recommends that, just like doctors do, you follow the following four-step process (explained in details in Chapter 5):

1. **The diagnosis:** This is the process by which you keenly observe your suffering in order to identify its cause

2. **The cause:** This is what brings out suffering as diagnosed by you.

3. **The treatment:** This is the process you follow in ending your suffering, known as Eightfold.

4. **The recovery:** This is the state at which you are fully treated or liberated from your suffering.

The Eightfold Path

The Eightfold Path, otherwise known as "the Middle Way" due to its avoidance of extremities of self-indulgence and self-torment consists of cultivating virtuousness, serenity and wisdom.

This Eightfold Path consists of;

1. Right View/Understanding – Right view is about having the right perspective that reflects the truth about reality.

2. Right Intention/Thought - Right intent is about embracing compassion, loving-kindness, and renunciation of all that leads to attachment to selfish desires.

3. Right Speech – Right speech is about uttering words that are gentle, kind, honest, meaningful, and with good intent.

4. Right Effort/Virtue – Right effort/virtue is about endeavoring to engage your effort towards non-violence, sexual responsibility, and respect for the Five Commandments (Five Precepts)

5. Right Livelihood – Right livelihood is about earning a just living by means of work that does not lead to harmful exploitation of oneself or others.

6. Right Action – Right action is about taking action that does not result into causing harm to oneself and others. It is taking action that honors the Five Commandments.

7. Right Mindfulness – Right mindfulness is about being consciously aware of your being, the nature of beings, and the nature of things.

8. Right Concentration – Right concentration is meditative concentration that brings you peace, deep unification with your nature of being, and purity of mind.

By following these Eightfold Paths, you are able to achieve a high degree of maturity. It is this high degree of maturity that enables you to become aware of the true nature of existence through perfect wisdom and unshakable liberation of which both are gained from deeper insight and experience.

The Five Precepts (Five Commandments)

Through the practice of Right Speech, Action, and Livelihood, which constitutes the training in Virtue or Morality, the following five precepts are honored:

1. Do not kill (Respect life) – Thus, you should not deliberately and unnecessarily cause death of any living being.

2. Do not steal (Respect other people's property) – thus, you should not intentionally convert another person's property into your own.

3. Do not commit adultery (Respect your own pure nature) – Thus avoid engaging in all forms of sexual misconduct or violence such as e.g. prostitution or cheating.

4. Do not offer false testimony (Respect your integrity) – you should not lie and never compromise your virtues for the sake of bearing false witness.

5. Do not corrupt your mind (Respect your conscience) – Thus, you should not take intoxicating substances or engage in addiction of all forms that seeks to impair your own conscience. Your mind is a sponge. Everything you feed it with, it will give back in some other form. Respect yourself feeding your mind only with fine and valuable things. Respect your time, it is very limited. You can spend your days curing hangovers in front of TV, browsing social media, or playing video games all the time, which will eventually make you miserable - or you can spend it creating value, helping others, playing instruments, doing sports, or reading books. Chose wisely.

"Nothing can harm you as much as your own thoughts unguarded."

"We are shaped by our thoughts; we become what we think. When the mind is pure, joy follows like a shadow that never leaves." - Gautama Buddha

Chapter 4: Karma, Rebirth and Reincarnation

"When a bird is alive, it eats ants.

When the birth is dead, ants eat the bird.

One tree makes a million match sticks.

Only one match stick needed to burn a million trees.

Time and Circumstance can change at any moment.

Do not devalue or hurt anyone in life. You many be powerful this time, but remember: Time is more powerful than you. So be good and do good." –

Unknown

Karma is one of those terms that have been frequently talked about, yet so often misunderstood. The theory of Karma is a core doctrine in Buddhism. Here, I will, albeit briefly, elaborate on it.

What is Karma?

In the simplest terms, Karma is the state of mind that arises when people act. It is the intent that precedes an action.

The Law of Karma

The law of Karma is very simple: every cause has an effect. The law of Karma is thus based on the cause-and-effect relationship between your intent and its outcomes. "A good cause, a good effect; a bad cause, a bad effect".

The Fallacies of Karma

Since karma is rather a foreign word to so many in the West, it one of the most abused terms. There are so many fallacies or misconceptions about karma. Common ones are:

1. That someone's karma is like fate and cannot be changed.
2. That those who are suffering must not be helped since it is their karma.
3. That the poor must be left poor since it is their karma.
4. That those who appear rich, beautiful, and wealthy are better off spiritually than those who are not since this is the result of their karma.

The Truths About Karma

To dispel the fallacies, it is important that the following truths about karma should be understood:

1. The power to change karma **rests within us.**
2. We have a **responsibility** to do all that we can to **mitigate suffering in the world.**

3. **Compassion** is the best karma you can cultivate within yourself.

4. The way to ending bad karma is by **embracing good karma.**

"All that we are is a result of what we have thought, it is founded on our thoughts and made up of our thoughts." – Guatama Buddha

Karma begets Karma

The more you embrace good intent into your actions the more you kick out bad intent. The outcome of this good intent motivates you (or rather brings a rebirth) of good intents. This becomes the rebirth of good karma and in essence the purifying effect of good karma.

The converse is also true. Your bad intent yields bad actions and further bad intents. Thus, instead of purifying you, the bad karma makes you impure and unhappy.

What is Rebirth?

Karma begets Karma - this is the essence of rebirth. Rebirth simply refers to the perpetuity of the karmic tendencies. Thus, if you have good karmic tendencies, they will bring forth new good karmic tendencies and unless you disrupt it by bad karma, this process of good karmic tendencies will continue ad infinitum and you will contribute to better being of this world and yourself.

"We are the heirs of our own actions." – Guatama Buddha

What is the relationship between Karma and rebirth?

Karma and Rebirth are simply a cause-and-effect relationship. The effect is called "Vipaka". Karma begets Karma through a process of rebirth. Thus, rebirth is the process of bringing forth new Karma. Your good deeds and intentions bring more goodness into your life, while the bad ones bring bad events and emotions.

What is Reincarnation?

Reincarnation is the continuity of the soul after death of the body. Hindus believe that once you die, your soul goes into another body after your death, depending on your deeds. Thus, if you did good, thus good karma, your soul moves into better being after your death. However, if you had bad karma, your soul transmutes into a worse being.

Which way for the Buddhists: Rebirth or Reincarnation?

Unfortunately, new students of Buddhism are often misled to believe that Rebirth and Reincarnation mean one and the same thing. They do not. Buddhism does not recognize reincarnation. Reincarnation is based on the immortality of the soul. Buddhists holds that the soul, just as the body disperses into various constituent elements of nature. Thus, Buddhism does not believe in transmigration of the soul.

Rather, they do believe in continuity of karma (good intents) from one life to another. Your bad karma, on the other hand, creates ignorance and unsatisfied desires that cause rebirth – something that happens from moment to moment (also after death) and can be described as self-imprisonment in suffering. Rebirth can be stopped.

"The constant state of flux, renewal and metabolic change that we experience physically (birth, old age, sickness, and death) and in our minds (the forming, existing, changing and ceasing of thoughts) are what we call the wheel of rebirth." - Master Hsing Yun

So what happens after the death according to Buddhists?

There's a nice Zen story of the disciple asking the Zen master: "What happens after death, master?"

And the master says: "I don't know"

And the disciple says: "How come? Aren't you a master?"

And the master replies: "Yes, but I'm not a dead one"

What you should know is that the Buddha himself was not keen on speculating about the beginning of this world or about afterlife, because he knew that no human being could ever be certain how life began and what happens when we die. Buddha never considered himself a God or any godly creature and was of the opinion that instead of speculating about things we can never be really sure of, it is better to deal with the problems we face everyday and make our lives (and the lives around us) better.

There's even a possibility that Buddha would say "That's not important at all", because what Buddhism focuses on is present moment, the only moment in which you can change your life and be happy

Did you know that in seven years' time your body changes all of its cells, and so to speak – physically - after that time you are an entirely new person? Buddha once said: "Every moment you are born, decay, and die." He was speaking about the illusion of "self" renewing itself. Speak about carrying anything over from one life to another after death – nothing is even carried from one minute to another. Your emotions and thoughts constantly change and so do the chemicals and neurotransmitters in your body when they're reacting with each other. You lose your hair and skin cells to grow new ones, your face and body is constantly transforming every day, even though you can't see it. The Buddha teaches that your permanent "self" (your personality or consciousness) is nothing but an illusion created by your senses, ideas, conceptualizations, beliefs, and values. Tell me where's the child you used to be? Where are your beliefs about the monsters from under the bed or your favorite activities such as playing with your blocks on the carpet? Where's that little fragile body? What's linking the actual "you" with that child, apart from your name and memories? There's a rebirth in every single second.

There are only two constant things in this world: change and death. After you notice that this is true through practicing meditation, you will be no longer be afraid of death, which is the most natural thing on this planet, and what's more, you won't be overly concerned with the future, but anchored in the present moment, as it's everything that you have ever had and will ever have. The very moment you experience that the idea of permanent metaphysical "I" is an illusion, you will stop suffering and cease to inflict suffering to others.

Just like clouds in the sky, forms appear and dissolve every moment. That applies both to psychical as physical forms in this world. Did you know that 99.9999999999999% of the atom is an empty space? That means that according to physics, you are 99.9999999999999% empty, and everything else that you perceive as solid is almost totally empty too. More than that, about 65% of your body is Oxygen; the majority of our bodies is water and moreover - we contain extremely large amounts of energy inside us. Are we solid?

The Earth is moving around the Sun at the speed of sixty seven thousand miles per hour, not to mention the speed of surface movement and the speed of our Solar system rotating around the center of our galaxy at the speed of four hundred ninety thousand miles per hour. And yet we perceive it stands still. Everything is an illusion.

There are the radio and WiFi waves in the air, the Internet, the Earth's electromagnetism, space radiation, and many other phenomena that we can't even see or sense at all. There's even the theory in quantum physics that all the Universe is just a big hologram and it's just a projection of a two-dimensional surface. Nevertheless, what physicist know for sure is that the information can NEVER be lost in the Universe. It must be still somewhere accessible to us. This is exactly what Buddha said a long time before any quantum physics research started; no information and no energy is ever lost in this world. What's real (the energy that animates you, the "spirit") can never be annihilated – you can't lose it, you ARE it. This is why the concept of death can't be applied to reality. This life is a wave, and at some point it will return to the Ocean, and so we will. Almost all the suffering comes from wrong perceptions of ourselves and the reality. If you meditate profoundly, you will feel that such ideas like existence and non-existence, or coming and going, are false notions. If you touch the reality, you can realize that "suchness" (Tathatā) – the ultimate existence – is free from being and non-being. If you are obsessing over death, it means that you just have wrong perceptions of it.

Buddhism teaches about Nirvana - the end of all misery and the ultimate goal often described as "the capacity of removing misunderstanding". Nirvana allows you to remove the wrong perceptions and fear of death and non-being. There's a transformation, a continuation, but there's no death - you can't be something and then become nothing. The ideas such as death should be removed with constant practice of meditation and following Buddha's principles.

I personally believe that when you die, in the last few moments, you experience yourself as a consciousness free of form. There's a certainty that death is just an illusion, just like the form that is dissolving, the one you were identifying yourself with so stubbornly. There's a feeling that everything is all right and you're just returning to where you came from.

What I really like about Buddhism is that it does not recognize eternal damnation. I've never believed that human beings could condemn themselves (or be condemned by a supreme being) to eternal punishment and suffering for their impurity, with no possibility of further redemption at all. If you think about it deeply, it comes out as the cruelest and sadistic concept ever invented. Even the most atrocious horror movies and stories seem like "Casper the Friendly Ghost" compared to that popular prospect.

Even though I have a Catholic Christian background, I used to go to church, confess my sins, and more than that - had spent few years as an acolyte when I was a boy - I could never really buy the concept of Loving Father accepting such maniacal cruelty - even when speaking about the worst criminals. I believed that even the worst "energy" that derived from the most evil actions should deplete eventually, just like the "energy" coming from good deeds. Unchanging eternity somehow made no sense to me (maybe I was born with the Buddhist mind?). This never appealed to me as justice of any kind and I spent countless hours talking to my parents, priests, monks and sitting in libraries - reading many theological books, both Christian and Muslim. I was looking for the answers very hard because that belief wasn't going along with my view of this world and my idea of God. I could not never-ever believe that any supreme, infinitely intelligent, and loving being could allow the existence of eternal hell. The few answers ("that's God's mystery" was never much of an answer to me) that I found just stated that we were the ones going away from God's purifying love and that He couldn't do anything to save us if we chose to waste our souls, as He didn't want to break our free will he had once gave to us... but honestly, it never made any sense to me at all. I always imagined it just like a hypothetical scene where a father sees his beloved son drizzling himself with gasoline, setting on fire, jumping out of the skyscraper's window - and yet remains passive. "If he wants to jump, let him jump" – the father says – "he has a free will, doesn't he? I can't stop him from suicide, otherwise I would have enslaved him". Seems legit? Maybe to some, but not to me.

I hope you don't get offended by my view here, mind you that it is my personal experience and opinion. On the other hand, I found a few

Catholic priests who believed that hell was empty because God's love was so strong that he couldn't allow for this kind of cruelty.

Well, there are numerous (looooots of!) Buddhist sects and each has slightly different beliefs, but what most of them believe is that there is an existence in plural realms in this universe: there is hell filled with depraved men, then dimension of hungry ghosts (similar to the Western ghost stories about lonely spirits that can't find their peace), animals (beasts), Asuras (very aggressive, fighting demon-like beings with a state of mind similar to a violent human with overgrown ego), human beings, Bodhisattvas – enlightened beings destined to stay on this planet to teach others how to attain enlightenment, Pratyekas – enlightened beings (Buddha's), and Sravka's – Buddha's disciples.

As you've noticed, there's a concept of hell as well - but it's not eternal. You can stay there for thousands of years, or maybe even eons, depending on your deeds and intents - but then, eventually, you become cleansed. Some believe that if someone's Karma is better, they're going to be reborn as human beings again, and though they won't keep their old memories (maybe just tiny glimmers and intuition), they will "be given" the Karma from their former life (the rebirth of Karma) and will have to go all of their mistakes again, until their Karma gets better, they gain understanding by following the Noble Eightfold Path and thus become enlightened - so that they can eventually cease this continuous circle of rebirth (which is unable to fully satisfy and produces pain) and finally rest in the big calm and bliss of Nirvana.

What I personally think is that these realms shouldn't be taken - so to speak – religiously and literally. Buddhism is about rationality, and these realms are difficult to be personally investigated and understood very seriously in our modern times. More than that, Buddhism traditionally teaches that there's no soul (anattā) that can transmigrate into another body, so one can't literally be reborn as, say, a cat or an obnoxious spider (yuck!).

You are not a separate being with a separate soul, but you are ONE with the Universe, with all-being, with "suchness". Imagine yourself as an unrestricted, limitless space. You are it. So rebirth is just a dance of forms appearing and dissolving, another illusion and another change. You are none of them and yet you are interconnected with everything. But you have to admit that - it's not too easy to understand until one starts meditating deeply and following the Buddha's teachings. Unfortunately, human beings are unable to speak the truth – just the words that describe the truth – and the words are so often misguided and futile.

What you need to know is that Buddha gave more than eighty thousand teachings during his entire life, and he always used to adjust them to his students' and listeners' spiritual and mental capabilities. The idea of these realms was probably created as a parable – similar to the Biblical ones that Jesus used to preach so often. Imaginative universal images created for people to understand the truth about "the nature of things" better. They were to be used also as a moral example – I can imagine that simple, rural Asian settlers from 500 B.C were scared of being reborn as animals, which probably restricted them from acting like animals and allowed them to live in peace. That also helped them to understand other important truths about life and human relations as well.

I hold that no matter if one believes in hell and heaven, or in continuous rebirth in these realms until Nirvana, they should be viewed as psychological conditions we are pushing ourselves in, caused by our good or bad karma. Moreover, I believe that each of these realms contains all the other realms inside. So as a human being you could be just listening to your bodily needs and acting like a wild animal/beast (sex or porn addiction, overeating, alcohol abuse etc.), you could have an unsatisfied appetite for fame, popularity, relationships, or love, which would make you more like a hungry ghost, you could be gradually pushing yourself to hell through selfishness or maybe walk the noble path of compassion and meditation, and become calm and happy like the Buddha himself. Also as an enlightened being (Buddha), you would have to know how "the hell on Earth" or how a state of unsatisfied hunger for something looks to be able to go into it in order to understand and help your principles.

And you should also notice how the animals so often act more "humanly" and morally than we use to.

Of course there's more to that when it comes to afterlife and karma, but this is just an e-book that is meant to be short and informative, and if I was to expand on every aspect of e.g. Tibetan or Zen Buddhism alone, it would take me at least few hundred pages. I just briefly presented you the idea so that you can see what I (and few hundred millions of other Buddhists) believe in.

More than that, you can read the Tibetan "Bardo Thodol" – also known by Westerners as the "Tibetan Book of Dead" – either the version translated by Walter Evans-Wentz's or by the Tibetans – it describes the experiences that consciousness freed from human body has after death. It is strikingly similar to many near-death testimonies of people who survived severe accidents (light in the tunnel, overview of the entire life, floating over one's body, presence of good and loving energy etc.). It is also a bit congenial with Egyptian book of Dead, Kabbalistic conceptions, and Taoism, but on the other hand - it's not really consistent with traditional Buddhism if you'd like to take it literally. But hey, you are the one who should find your own way, so approach this knowledge and philosophy however you want!

Take it as your belief, or not – but according to Buddha - you shouldn't unless it makes sense to you on a personal level and you can find the truth in it. Although you may feel different, that's one of few concepts that make any sense to me and it gives me hope.

If you still feel that you'd like to reflect more about rebirth, you can read this interesting essay:

http://www.accesstoinsight.org/lib/authors/bodhi/bps-essay_46.html.

Chapter 5: Where Do I Start?

Indeed, you are welcome to the world of Buddhism. The practice of Buddhism is such that it transcendent all bounds of religions. Yes, there are those who choose to take Buddhism as religion. You don't need to take it as such for it only becomes your religion when you make it to be. Buddhism is about ending suffering through enlightenment and eventually attaining Nirvana – that state of no bad perceptions, of eternal bliss, joy peace and harmony, where serenity reigns in abundance.

Where should you start? Well, first of all you must know that life is whole and as such it cannot be compartmentalized into material life, religious life, spiritual life and the rest. By gaining this knowledge so would you awaken to the universal truths about suffering that are not held hostage to false beliefs, practices, and traditions. To gain greater insight, take the initial step to walk the path to ending suffering. And as you walk, you will grow the urge to learn more and finally flourish as a person. Buddhism is about whole life without compartmentalization. Remember: there is no distinction between spiritual life and daily life, no distinction between body and soul, and thus, just as they both come, so do they both leave.

Thich Nhat Hanh once said "It is not important whether you walk on water, or in space, the true miracle is to walk on earth." This gives a reflection as to how ordinary Buddhism is. It is about you in your own ordinary ways. To Buddhism loving-kindness and compassion are the greatest miracle a human being can perform.

"If we could see the miracle of a single flower clearly our whole life would change." – Gautama Buddha

Do Awake

To awaken is to become aware, which is the sole purpose of truth. **The greatest truth is that spiritual life and daily life are one and the same.** Thus, practicing kindness and compassion in your daily life is indeed leading a daily spiritual life.

To awaken is to become aware of what is happening within and around you. Always ask yourself "why I am doing/saying that I'm doing/saying right now?" and "how am I doing that? I'm here and present? I'm one hundred percent committed to what I'm doing? If not, why is that? What's the reason my thoughts are somewhere else?" Ask yourself where you are going in your life. Where have your past decisions taken you?

Another important question that you should be aware of is connected to the people around you. Always take a moment to think about what your words or actions will do to these people and how will they react. Mind you that what you do and say also affects your own emotions through other people's reactions, so that your unwholesome words or actions can create a vicious circle for your entire environment.

You should also apply this practice of presence to even the most trivial things, like brushing your teeth, eating breakfast, or taking a walk. You should always be focused on what you're doing **right now.** You may find yourself surprised how much there's to discover about yourself and about your life even in these little things. That's the only way to become present. If you're not present, you're simply wasting your life, because your life is here, it's now, it's in this very moment. There's no past, there's no future, yet – no one ever experienced "past" and no one ever experiences "future", because that's impossible (something you should really think about) - and the only moment for taking action to make your future happy and bright is **now** anyways.

I can't even count how many times I hit myself in the head or fell over on the icy road because I was everywhere in my thoughts but not there, living my real life. These trivial "countless mindless self-injuries" led me to see a bigger picture of my life. When I couldn't be mindful while cutting bread or washing my hands, how on earth could I be focused and concentrated on important aspects of my life? Obviously I couldn't. I was distracted from A to Z. Then I realized how faraway I used to be when meeting my friends and spending time with my family – I would think about my job or business or another future plans, but then, back home, I would think about my friends instead of doing my job. That was a big nonsense and a waste. And so then I started from focusing on the smallest everyday tasks and things. I started asking myself these simple but important questions. Everything's changed now.

You must not only observe but also engage in truthful inquiry of everything around you. More so, you must question your very own beliefs, your very own traditions, words of others, words of 'supernatural beings', authority of ancient scriptures, elders, priests, teachers, etc. That's the only way to find YOUR, not someone else's, truth. Buddhism teaches us that the world is not dualistic. It's not black and white. There is universal truth in Nirvana, in the enlightenment, in "suchness", but you can't be given the truth directly, you can't just obtain it without experiencing it. The Buddha shows you the way, but you have to walk it on your own.

My personal philosophy is to always be abandoning all the beliefs I can't defend from my own and others' attacks. I often watch movies or read books that are totally against my perceptions and beliefs, and can even be offensive to me at some levels. So often I feel that curious kind of "pain" inside me, whenever I read that something I believed in was not true, didn't work, and made no sense. That always leads me into further inquiries.

If I can't defend a particular belief under a crossfire of difficult questions and problems, if there's a crack on the glass that is going further and I can't do anything about that, if I can't explain to myself why I believe so, if I don't see how that's going to serve me and the people I love – I just quit the philosophy or a certain belief. At the times when I was particularly in love with backpacking, I really enjoyed engaging in discussions (often in people's cars when I was hitchhiking, or in planes) about how I was irresponsible, how the traveling was going to make me catch a tropical disease and eventually make me broke and unhappy...how I should've never quit my job and how a university education was the most important thing in the world.

That way, and only that way, I could feel that everything I was doing made just perfect sense to me. I could strengthen my beliefs and be sure that the path I chose was perfect for me. It allowed me to stand firm on my own ground without any distracting doubts. I could never understand why so many Muslims and Christians (say, my parents) didn't want to read atheistic books such as "The God Delusion", why marijuana smokers didn't want to watch any serious academic medical testimonies and reports other than "how tetrahydrocannabinol is a panacea medicine for every kind of sickness" (not that I have anything against them), or how Buddhists didn't want to read books stating that Buddhism is just a hippie-outdated kind of pointless B.S and how it's totally useless in serious people's everyday life.

If you can't defend your own beliefs, WHY on earth would you stick to them? It's like being in a relationship with a person you don't like that doesn't like you either, who is rude and unattractive to you... or building a high ladder out of rotten sticks. The rungs have to be solid!

You are going to step up on them!

Thus, you must empty your mind off any held beliefs, attitudes, and prejudices that you cannot support. Yet, you must do this in the most sober, respectful, tolerant and non-violent way. Only by discovering that a given belief is an affirmation of your very own experience and discovery should you give it a chance - not to get fixed onto it, but as the knowledge that you must keep on interrogating.

Do Walk the Path to Ending Suffering

The path to ending suffering is to experience the Four Noble Truths. This path encompasses a four-step process;

1. Diagnose your suffering: Pain is a reminder of your very own suffering. It may be spiritual, psychological, mental, emotional, social, or physical. Each of these pains is an alarm that alerts you of the need to do something - yes, diagnose your suffering.

2. Determine the cause of your suffering: The cause of your suffering rests in deep in your mind. Yes, the external circumstances may arouse your stimuli, but how you choose to experience it makes the difference between you suffering or not. Thus, the cause of your suffering is the intent or Karma that you've embraced in your mind.

3. Discover the path to recovery: The path to your recovery is that which leads to a complete end of all your sufferings - your ultimate attainment of enlightenment.

4. Carry out your treatment: The only lasting cure to your suffering is enlightenment. Like any cure, it is administered in gradual dosage. The dosage for ending suffering comprises of the milestones you undertake on the Noble Eightfold Path.

Let me know show you a practical example of a process which can be used in this context. If you're unhappy, you should inquire into the one who is unhappy. What do I mean by that?

Let's say that your unhappiness is caused by a particular relationship. Your action should not necessarily be to change the relationship itself (although you might really want to do it as well if it's really not going anywhere), but to turn towards yourself, the "I" who is unhappy. So you ask yourself: "What is this "I"?" Because the unhappiness that "I" feels is not necessary being caused by just this relationship - "I" has also felt exactly the same unhappiness at other times in your life for completely different reasons.

It was the same feeling, but had numerous different causes. If it's caused by lots of different things, no single thing can be a cause of this happiness. So that maybe you should question the "I" who is so often unhappy, because that's exactly the one constant that is always the same in all of these experiences? The causes may change, but the "I" is always the same "I".

You use the word "I" many times during the day, so think of it now - what are you exactly referring to? You are probably referring to the person you used to call "I", that is your body, the collection of your memories, feelings, thoughts and perceptions, right?

So then you notice: "my thoughts are always coming and going...but I'm not always coming and going. I'm just aware of my thoughts. I thought I was my thoughts, but actually that's not the case". Then just observe the thoughts – feel as they come and go. You will see that you are just observer of your thoughts. So often you don't even have to continue them at all if you don't want to. They are constantly changing. You are not them.

Then proceed to your emotions - of being lonely guilty, sad etc. You will also notice that your feelings appear and disappear, but you- your awareness – is still there. Let's say that you were upset in the morning, but you're just OK in the afternoon – so that emotion went away – do you feel that part of yourself vanished too? No. You're still there. So you can't really identify yourself with your emotions.

Then you do the same with your sensations – you can pinch yourself or brush your hair and then stop– they also come and go.

Your images, the sights and the sounds you hear – all these appear and disappear, but you don't.

So then you come to interesting realization – you thought that you were a "package" of your thoughts, feeling, emotions and sensations – but then you notice that they are constantly changing, coming and going – and you're something separate from them.

You are aware of them.

The only thing that has always been there in your life is this "observer" who has always been aware of all these emotions, sensations, thoughts, feelings and the whole world around. A witness.

So then you start redefining of what you used to call "I". Then you can ask yourself again: "what is this sensation of unhappiness"?

That's not "I" who is unhappy. The "I" is just perfectly peaceful, unlimited space of awareness, through which all these emotions and feelings constituting "unhappiness" go.

So then you may become intrigued and ask yourself "what is that present awareness that is always there, that knows my experiences but is not made of these experiences, which is not made of thoughts, feelings, perceptions, sensations"? That may result in changing your focus from all these passing sensations, the "package", and paying more attention to the present and aware "I", the background, the unrestricted space, the essence of your being. Who is aware of that? Well, it is aware of itself. It is aware of your experience. It is this "I" that is aware of itself. Then, you should start looking on yourself instead of your thoughts, feelings.

And then, finally, you may turn back to your feelings again, and notice that they're long gone and your unhappiness is nowhere to be found.

The cause of unhappiness and suffering is mistaking yourself - the "I" - with the train of emotions and feelings – and as long as you do that, you will have a bad relationship with yourself, so to speak – suffering is misunderstanding your true essence and the nature of things.

Take the Ultimate Responsibility of Ending Suffering Upon You;

1. Take steps to understand the three universal truths
2. Take steps to understand the four noble truths
3. Take steps to understand and practice the eight-fold paths
4. Keep the five commandments wholly

"Peace comes from within. Do not seek it without." - Gautama Buddha

Take Steps to Understand the Three Universal Truths

The following are three important universal truths that you must embrace in your practice of Buddhism.

1. Nothing is lost in the universe – this is a reminder that you should not grieve overly due to your loss of whatever you may have attached yourself to. Everything that do exist including you, your loved ones, and all your belongings are part and parcel of this one indivisible universe. Therefore, the universe as a whole loses nothing. Not even your death is a loss to the universe, for upon your death, your body returns to the various elements of the universe from which it originated from. Christians express this as "from dust to dust and from ash to ash" thus, from where you came from so shall you go back to – the universe. Yet, you won't go anywhere since you came from nowhere, for you are not somewhere, except you being the whole universe. So, of course you will be sad when you lose something or someone – that's perfectly normal and sane for us in this earthly life when forms change their appearance - and the point's not being in becoming a emotionless robot (rather on the contrary!) - but don't torture yourself over that. Everything's going to be just all right as there's no real distinction between all human beings, we really are all just one big whole.

2. Everything changes – Nothing in this universe is static. Even the earth that seems static is on the move, hills and valleys

come and go, oceans form and disappear, rivers flow and dry, stars appear and implode, beings gain life and then die, etc. Thus, you must embrace change as inevitable. You must be open to change in your life.

3. Every cause has an effect – this teaches you that nothing happens without a cause. Yet every cause that results into your suffering is an effect of your intent, or Karma. The best way to understand the cause of your suffering is to understand the Four Noble Truths.

Take Steps to Understand the Four Noble Truths

The Four Noble Truths are truths about our suffering;

1. There is suffering and suffering is common to all – Suffering is not what happens to us but what we intend, say, and do about what happens to us. Thus, your intent, words, and actions are not confined to you but they flow like ripples from the vibration of your thought, word, or deed in a restful ocean, causing disturbance across the ocean.

2. We are the cause of our own suffering – we cause our own suffering by the bad karma that we cultivate within our minds.

3. We can end suffering by doing away with that which causes suffering. We can end suffering by cultivating good intents. Good intents, or rather, good karma will enable us to seek enlightenment about our suffering and thus be able to end it.

4. The path to end suffering is enlightenment and everyone can be

enlightened. The path to ending suffering is that which brings you to the realization of the existence of the Eightfold Paths.

Take Steps to Understand and Practice the Eight-fold Paths

The following are the Eightfold Paths that you should endeavor to practice in your daily life.

1. **Right View/Understanding:** Having the right view/understanding is to have the right perspective of circumstances, experiences and nature of things and beings. Having right view enables you to keep off pretenses and false illusions, thus being able to see things as they truly are. This right view enables you not only to keep the 'Five Commandments' wholly but also to gain enlightenment. Right view enables you to understand the cause of human suffering; the existence of birth, aging, sickness and death; the existence of hate, greed, and delusion.

   Right view reflects light onto the other seven paths, thus allowing you to actualize them. Right view is the knowledge about suffering, its cessation and the way to cessation. There are two primary types of views;

   - Mundane view: Mundane view is that view which you achieve by looking at things through tainted lenses. These lenses are polluted by prejudices, prior inexhaustible experiences, beliefs, taboos, previous teachings, etc.

- Supra-mundane view: Supra-mundane view is that view which you achieve by looking at things through clear and untainted lenses. Thus, these lenses are not corrupted by all these things from the former bullet point.

Right view enables you to understand the moral law of Karma; every action has its own karmic effects (reaction). Thus:

- Unwholesome action/effort will yield unwholesome outcome.

- Every thing that arises so shall it cease.

- The degree of your ignorance is proportionately responsible for the arising of your suffering. Thus, your ending of this degree of ignorance is also proportionately responsible to that extent of the cessation of your suffering.

- The arising of selfish intents is proximately proportional to the arising of your suffering and the elimination of these selfish intents is proximately proportional to the cessation of your suffering.

The aim of Right View is to enable you to clear your path off confusion, misconceptions and delusions. You should be able to exercise flexibility in your perspective without being held hostage to dogmatic positions. It is only by this kind of Right View that you gain knowledge that liberates you rather than enslaving you.

2. **Right Intention/Thought:** For you to achieve good karma, you must cultivate right intent. Only by you cultivating right intent can you experience positive rebirth. Yes, this agrees well with Jesus teachings about being 'born again'. This right intent leads you to develop compassion, empathy, and renunciation of all attachments to all possessions that cause you suffering. The right intention can be also understood as a constant drive or a strong will to get rid of suffering – to change yourself, your life, and to alter your current unhappy situation or state of mind. With the right intention you also ultimately win over your fear of losing job, money, ending bad relationships, being lonely or even sick. With right intention, you are not unnecessarily frightened anymore and ultimately committed to change your life, even if there's a possibility that you will become different. What you may need to cultivate in order to maintain the right intention is a strong sense of urgency to overcome your suffering.

3. **Right Speech:** You should endeavor to utter words of truth. Words that are clear to understand, soft to listen to, and geared towards fostering harmony. Thus, to achieve the five commandments, your words should not be slanderous as to cause you lose respect for your integrity. They should also not demean the other person such as to cause you lose respect for

life. Similarly, they should not be words of perjury as to cause you lose respect for your conscience. Always be conscious of your self-talk. It is VERY important. I often used to "whip myself" when I failed to complete a task that I had promised myself I would complete, or when the outcome was different than planned – I would punish myself verbally in my mind. I thought that it was my helpful "self discipline", but my psychotherapist at the time made me see that it was just me inflicting suffering and harm to myself. I used to do that even when I really couldn't change anything and was on the lost position from the start. The words you use in your mind are **extremely** important. They should express self-love like your life depended on it, but never self-hatred! You need to control your imagination and your language. Your mind is a system and it can be programmed - this can't be expressed enough - it is a sponge. Whenever you want to "punish" yourself in your own mind – just stop! It won't do you any good, just make you unhappy. You should also definitely stop gossiping and never be looking for sensationalism. Whenever you comment on someone else's relationships, bank account, car, wife, or even lawn, you do nothing but poison your own life. Again, you should avoid words of connivance that could make you illegitimately gain someone else's property. When it comes to relationships, your words should not be words of enticement as to cause you to ensnare someone else's wife/husband, and as such to cause you to lose respect for your own pure nature.

"The tongue like a sharp knife... Kills without drawing blood." - Gautama Buddha

4. **Right Action:** This entails you not taking any action that may lead you to violating the Five Commandments. You should not take any action that leads to loss of human life. You should not take an action that unnecessarily leads to lose of an animal or plant. You should remember that human beings are like mirrors. We are even equipped with "mirror neurons" responsible for observing and copying other people's actions and feeling what they feel. Have you ever noticed how easy it is to become upset when you are waiting for an exam (even if you're fully prepared) or an interview in a room full of other nervous people? Or how contagious laugh and yawning can be? That's it. So that whenever your actions towards people around you (even the ones you dislike) are supportive and full of love, the reaction will be alike. If your actions are bad, that's the response you will get. Your words and actions are very important ingredients of your everyday happiness, and yet so often overlooked and neglected.

5. **Right Effort/Virtue:** You should channel your effort to keep off bad karma (wrong intent), wrong speech, and harmful actions. By right effort, you should be able to:

  - Eschew the unwholesomeness that has not arisen in you.

This simply means that you should avoid investing your effort in those endeavors that comes to you as incomplete manifestations of truth. Thus, what is not completely truthful should be shunned from your effort. This helps you from embracing beliefs from others which are not completely truthful.

- Let go off your attachment to the unwholesomeness that has arisen in you. If a thought has come to you and it is a thought that is not a complete manifestation of truth, and whose truth cannot be manifested by your meditation, let go off it. This helps you to stop creating beliefs about that which is not completely truthful.

- Nurture the wholesomeness that has not arisen in you. This means that you should accept and nurture truth from others and embrace it wholesomely no matter how much inconvenience or pain it may appear to cause to your ego, for it the only way to become enlightened and thus end your suffering.

- Nurture the wholesomeness that has arisen in you. It also makes you trust yourself.

You should also be determined to protect yourself from vicious ideas and actions even coming to your mind. You can help yourself by feeding your mind with quality content and activities, such as reading good books, doing sports, playing instruments, watching good movies that you can learn something from, and listening to good music that makes you calm and happier, everyday meditation, contact with nature, healthy relations and staying away from any violence, gossips, or news and media/internet/digital overload.

Feeding your body with good, natural, healthy food instead of overly processed junk and sticking to rational diet will also surely help you as there's no real distinction between your mind and body. They are interlinked on every level.

6. **Right Livelihood:** You should earn your bread not by engaging in employment or business that violates the Five Commandments. Thus you should not engage in employment or business that leads to e.g.:

- Killing of animals and dealing with meat (doesn't mean that you should immediately dump your job if you work in butchery/ butcher shop and become homeless to live under a tree, but maybe you should reconsider your choices and develop new skills that will enable you to make a living differently).

- Scams – making money on people's naivety, credulity, stupidity, or even greed is not a good idea at all – believe me – it will all come back to you sooner or later.

- Manufacturing of addictive substances or drug dealing – I don't have to expand on that one if you have ever watched "Breaking Bad" – I personally think that this show is a great educative image of Good and Bad karma and the consequences that follow, especially if you take a look at all the lives that Walt's business took both directly and indirectly, and how much suffering he inflicted on people around him, chiefly to his own family. Of course that's just a TV show - obviously in reality that would be much, much worse.

- Weapons dealing – more or less as above.

- Poisonous substances

- Leads to enslavement of human beings either by forced labor, prostitution, or buying and selling of children – and even though this example may seem "hardcore" to you – this could also mean treating the people you've employed in the right way and with forbearance, even if they could be working better, and never to humiliate anyone.

It also means that in general you should be honest as an employee, employer or a self-employed person and in every other aspect of your life – with your family, friends, grocery shop workers, the people you are stuck with in a traffic jam (no need to call them names and punch your horn again and again, really...), and your neighbor's loud dog. This point can be very hard, but that's really big step bringing you closer to the real happiness and removing the mental poison you have maybe toxified yourself with.

7. **Right Mindfulness:** You must endeavor to clearly see things as they are - that comes down to your body, mind, and all the phenomena around you -- without becoming susceptible to ignorance, greed, avarice, etc. It is by practicing right mindfulness that you can embrace, nurture, and beget good karma (intent) and also become calm and wise in numerous different social or everyday life situations.

8. **Right Concentration:** Right concentration helps you to go deeper beyond the sequence of passing thoughts such that you are no longer influenced by cravings of the thought, and thus become a master of your own mind and will. It is the freedom from the roller coaster of conditional happiness-unhappiness, the fleeting emotions making you miserable that you identify yourself with. It is the blue sky free of clouds, a calm sea – the access to the unconditional happiness that has always been inside you. The Right Concentration can be achieved, for instance, through meditation.

Notice how the Eight-fold Paths is really interconnected with the whole society – it doesn't only underline the importance of individual conduct or behavior, but shows that, as Christopher McCandless noticed before his death: "happiness is only real when shared" – if you want to experience the real, unconditional happiness and meaningfulness, then you have to be a star that shines for other people; you have to be a good and large-hearted person. You have to be a source of inspiration and support your community on their on way to their own enlightenment. Remember that we are all interconnected. We are all one Universe. There's no "you". It is an illusion. Buddhism teaches you how empathy is extremely important on your way (and thus the whole world's way) to the ultimate happiness. And once you become enlightened, then you can be even better person and give even more support to the people around you.

To easily gasp the essence of these Eightfold Paths, I can summarize them under the following key categories:

- Wisdom – Right View, Right Intention

- Ethical Conduct - Right Speech, Right Action, Right Livelihood

- Concentration – Right Effort, Right Mindfulness, Right Concentration

Wisdom

Right Thought and Right Understanding are the key ingredients that bring forth wisdom. It is this wisdom that ends ignorance and pursuits for selfish desires. Thus, once you gain wisdom, your personality is transformed and thus you achieve boundless compassion and astounding serenity.

Solomon was considered the wisest and richest man of the Old Testament Bible. He is famously known to have requested to be granted wisdom by God, above everything else. He never requested for wealth, he never requested for power, but wisdom. Wisdom granted him everything else.

Ethical Conduct

Right Speech, Right Action, and Right Livelihood are the anchors upon which virtues and morality are held. These are the very practices upon the Five Commandments are achieved.

The greatest essence of all religious endeavors is to live an ethical life - a life free from 'sins'. This is what Abrahamic religions (Judaism, Christianity and Islam), Buddhism, Hinduism and others aim to achieve as the highest aspirations of an individual. In Buddhism we don't talk about "sins" per se (e.g. as deeds that are offensive to a Supreme Being), but more about actions and intentions that will poison your own life, hold you from enlightenment, and just make you and the people around you unhappy.

Concentration - the Practice of Meditation

Right Effort, Right Mindfulness and Right Concentration are achieved through the practice of Meditation. Meditation purifies the mind and enables you to achieve all the other Rights. Through meditation, you are able to break the crust and enter the core of inner stillness within which the well of purity resides and from you gather 'water of life' to nourish your insight.

Concentration is what Jesus referred to when he kept on calling his believers to give up every earthly pursuit for the glory of God, for the remission of their sins, and for their salvation. It is also what Islam practices during the holy month of Ramadan. It is what Buddhists practice during meditation.

Buddha stresses the importance of ethical conduct or virtue in attaining perfect Meditation. Thus, to Buddha, you cannot achieve perfect Meditation without perfecting the practice of virtue. Buddha also teaches that without practicing perfect Meditation, you cannot achieve that state of enlightenment. Without enlightenment you cannot enter Nirvana.

Unlike the way most Westerners view meditation as a mind-only activity, Buddha views meditation as part of the process to enlightenment and thus it cannot be achieved in isolation from right virtues. Hence, for you to meditate, you must not only cultivate the virtue of loving-kindness and compassion, you must also cultivate wisdom that will enable you to get rid of all those things that block the channels of right mindfulness.

Meditation is not ritualistic. It arises out of good intent. You may perform those rituals that help you advance this kind of concentration but they must not distract your intent.

Going to a quiet place where no one distracts you, getting rid of clutter from your surroundings and having a certain kind of posture are all geared towards creating that serene environment that can bring your mind to rest. It is in this condition of mind being at peace that you can make a deeper penetration into your inner being and the true nature of beings and things. Thus, your intent for meditation should be supreme to the form of meditation you are endeavoring to take.

If someone asked me about the best things I have come across my entire life, then "meditation" would be definitely one of my answers. I can't even express how deeply it can change you and your entire perception. Over the years (but even the first weeks) it's made me calm and collected, organized, focused, happier, and definitely less stressed (among many others, but there's no point in writing out half of the English dictionary). I was ultimately able to control myself and my reactions. Let me tell you this story as an example.

I can remember that I used to be extremely stressed anytime I got myself into situations that could possibly end up in a fight. Too many times I would just surrender, apologize for being alive, and runaway trembling, or retreat even when I shouldn't be retreating. Somehow my nervous system just couldn't handle that, even though I knew how to fight – not that I was a chicken-hearted version of Terminator, but I knew how to keep a guard and also few effective judo throws. Even though I have won few fights over the years, these situations were still too stressful for me.

Not longer than few weeks after I started practicing meditation, I had a date and I took that girl to one of the most popular clubs in my town, but it turned out that it was definitely too crowded that evening and there were hardly any free seats. We didn't feel like dancing and shouting all night and decided to go somewhere else - but she told me that she had to use ladies' room before. I knew her long enough to realize how much time it could take her to do her hair, improve make-up, and whatnot. It was late already and I was tired, but I noticed one last remaining seat by the table occupied by two guys.

I sat by the table, at the very end of the bench. After few seconds one of the guys turned to me and told me to kindly go somewhere else (while using all the curses and offenses available in English language). He was much bigger than me and angry, possibly on steroids. I was not touching them, I was not taking their personal space or even sitting close enough to hear them. I didn't even give them a look, facing another direction. I just wanted to sit there for few minutes as I was tired after work and gym, wait for the girl and then leave immediately. I told that kindly to the aggressive guy, but in reply he just told me what he would like to do with my face and my mother. Then, all of sudden, he grabbed my neck with his big hand, pulled my head to his forehead and started shouting that he would mutilate and kill me. Normally I would probably go gray and escape trough closed window, but I remained extremely calm instead, just like I was sitting on a grassy field in the mountains and playing with my dog. I still remained silent. He started pressing my neck harder and shouting even louder right into my face. Still, there was no stress at all in me.

Then I saw my hand going on his neck. I pressed it and said: "Yes, you can hit me if you want. Better do it right now. This club is full of cameras and bouncers, though. You will have no more that few seconds to do anything to me. Then they will come for you, throw you both out and that will be the end of this night's fun for and your friend. Believe me, you will never be allowed into this club again."

He released me and made a stupid face. Then he threw few adjectives again and grabbed my arm, but was too confused to do anything to me. Few seconds later my date appeared, took my hand and we left the club.

I hold that street fights are really stupid in general (you never even know who are you going to fight with) and should be averted at any cost (and that's the same opinion that every smart self-defense instructor has) and I think that being calm and in control is the best way to avoid them if there's such a possibility. Notice how often people get attacked only because they are scared and distracted.

After that experience, I never got too stressed with these situations again and because of my relaxed attitude no one ever hit or threatened me again, even when I had problems with deceitful thieves who stole my wallet at the shady narrow streets of Marrakech. It was just like I knew exactly what to say.

By no means I am suggesting that you should meditate and then put yourself in dangerous positions because you will become invincible, **but** the big calm was there for me also in many other life situations like job interviews, degree exams, meeting new people, dating (I once met a wonderful girl just by looking into her eyes and smiling gently while on the bus – I was never able to do that before regular meditation), money problems, or difficult and important decisions.

Meditation is one of the most powerful habits that you can establish in your life!

There are many different types of meditation and in this book I'm going to show you Mettā – the meditation of compassion and love which is very close to Buddhist philosophy of peace and forgiveness.

How To Practice Mettā Meditation

1. First of all – please take a moment to pick a place for your meditation. The best idea is to find one location where you can feel at peace and stick to it. For me it can be my bedroom or a bench in the nearby forest. The place should be silent. Get rid of your phone, laptop, tablet, and any electronic devices that could possibly distract you. Ask your family or friends not to disturb you for twenty minutes.

2. Sit in a comfortable position, you can also lie down if that won't make you sleepy. The posture of your meditation is up to you – it should be comfortable so that you can remain alert.

3. Close your eyes. Relax – take few deep breaths. Inhale and exhale calmly for a moment, until you feel that your body and mind "slowed down" a little bit.

4. Spend few moments relaxing all the tight spots and tensions in your body. You can also strongly tense (long enough to feel slightly tired - about fifteen seconds) and then relax muscles in these parts. You can also stretch for a moment before you even start the meditation. It is difficult to focus on meditation when your body is tired and wants your attention.

5. Now breathe deeply and with your eyes still closed wish yourself all the best like it's your birthday: harmony, success, health and wealth, the ability to understand your purpose and to follow it, to overcome all the difficulties you may be facing. You may be telling yourself: "May I be happy, may I be free of illness and injury, may I be healthy, may I be wealthy…" and so on. You also come up with rhymes to memorize your mantra better (yes, you can call it that). Repeat the phrase few times before you proceed further.

6. Then wish yourself ability to go of anxiety, greed, bad will, jealously, and other bad emotions or feelings: "May I resolve my anger, may I resolve my anxiety, may I resolve my bad will" etc.

7. Then wish yourself compassion, kindness, and bliss: "May I appreciate all my experiences, may I be thankful for my life, may I be friendly to myself, may I resolve my regrets".

8. You can also wish yourself: "May I cultivate wisdom in myself, may my skills multiply, may I be more patient".

9. The reason you should start this meditation with yourself is that it is extremely difficult (or impossible) to be kind to others when you don't know how to be kind to yourself. It is definitely impossible to really love other people when you don't love yourself in the first place. Some people feel like starting this meditation for others though, and that's OK as well, but it's easier to start with yourself as it calms the mind.

10. Now wish all of these things to the people that are important to you: family, friends, mentors etc. You can focus on each person, or the whole group. "May my family be happy, may my family be

healthy, may my family be blissful..." etc. Use the same phrases from the above "self-wishing" process.

11. Then proceed further and send your love and compassion using all these phrases to:

- People who you know, but are not close to you – they might be your neighbors, customers, your boss, the guy from the gas station etc.

- Then proceed to all the people you don't know – all the people walking down the streets, waiting in their cars next to you during traffic jams, people from other blocks and neighborhoods etc. – you can think both about particular people that you remembered and imagine their faces or about the whole group of people in general. This kind of practice helps you break the mental barrier that constitute the duality of "me" and "the rest" and teaches you compassion towards everyone.

- Then comes the most difficult part: the people that you dislike, the people who made you feel bad, your enemies and so on. Even though you may have problems with this kind of practice initially, remember:

"By holding on to anger you are like a man who wants to hit another and picks up a burning ember or excrement in his hand and so first burns himself or makes himself stink." - Visuddhimagga IX, 23.

Being angry and resentful does you no good – just poisons your own life. Ask any psychotherapist if you haven't experienced this truth yet.

If you still can't do it then again- go back to you and wish yourself peace, wisdom and forgiveness.

12. Should you feel distracted, change your posture and relax the tension from any tight part of your body again. If there any unpleasant thoughts arising, analyze them. Why are they appearing? In which parts of your body are they appearing? Are there any benefits of such emotions and thinking? What are the downsides? This kind of approach allows you to recognize these negative thoughts and emotions in the future. Then let go of these emotions and thoughts, take few deep breaths and if you feel that you may need it, return to focusing on yourself and wishing "May I be calm, may I resolve my resentments, may I be at peace".

13. Take chances to dissolve every tension or hardening that arises in your mind or in your body when you're thinking of someone you don't like or have negative thoughts about yourself.

14. You can also try to imagine your love towards the whole world and send your compassion and love to people from other countries, continents, to animals, plants, and the whole Universe. You can also use the words "I love you, thank you for everything".

15. After you finish, take few moments to relax again, just as in the beginning.

When you keep practicing Mettā, it gives you a great insight into how your social interactions are, how your mind operates, what are your hidden feelings and motives. You will also realize that there were lots of emotions in your body you had no idea ever existed and you will get definitely more patient over time.

There are also many different types of meditation.

For example – take a look at the cover of this book. This fractal-like thing is called "mandala". This is common practice among Vajrayana Buddhist monks, where they sandpaint big and complex mandalas. They often symbolize harmony, cleansing, and the order of the Universe. It usually takes the monks few hours or even few days/weeks, but soon upon completion the mandalas are destroyed. It teaches them detachment, great concentration, and also shows how all forms are impermanent. This is obviously just an example to stimulate your imagination (please don't create mandalas on your wife's favorite carpet!), but what I meant is that meditation can take many different forms.

It could even be a silent walk in the forest or park, where you listen to the birds and wind playing among the leaves, passively observing all the thoughts – not identifying with them, not labeling them, just letting go. Feeling the breeze on your skin. Feeling the sunbeam on your eyelids. Smelling the nature. Being present and aware.

A few years ago I had a wrong overall image of meditation in my mind and was sure that this kind of practice was good for Tibetan monks and teenage hippies, but not for regular working, busy people. Thankfully I met a friend who – while being an ordinary 'everyday normal guy' – struck me with his uncommon deep calm, peace, and positive attitude towards life's problems. From that moment on, I started learning how to meditate and practiced mindfulness everyday, and convinced myself how rich and profitable benefits of meditation really are.

I summed up all my experiences in this book:

http://www.amazon.com/dp/B00KQRU9BC/

I think that it's decent and easy to understand. If you want to make your life peaceful and successful, I recommend that you read it.

Keep the Five Commandments Wholly

I call the Five Precepts the Five Commandments, since without keeping them, you cannot achieve enlightenment. These Five Commandments are;

1. Respect life – To respect life is to understand that every life exists for a reason. Thus, you should not terminate the life of a human being. Furthermore, you may not unnecessarily and recklessly cause loss of life of other beings including plants. You should not slaughter an animal except for the need of meeting daily need for food and protection of your life. I used to be a keen hunter - a member of a game hunting club. I could visit almost any forest with my friends just to hunt down and shoot deer, boars, and the

like. I never used to do this for the need of meat (we saved and cooked the meat, but that was not a necessity, but our own whim— we had, of course, butcher shops at hand, right?), but just to have fun I have hunted down and killed an animal. From the time I started practicing Buddhism and meditation, I realized that I was wrong and stopped game hunting for good. Once I shot a roe-deer and then, when we were about to give it a closer look, drag to our pickup truck and talk about dividing its part for meat, we heard a sad cry. That was a baby roe we didn't notice before, hidden beneath a dense bush. Her skinny legs were shaking as she looked at us and the body. We killed her mother and left the poor animal alone in the wild. As soon as I realized that and heard the cry, I felt warm tears dropping down my cheeks. I felt shame that is impossible to even express and then started to cry myself like a little kid. I instantly remembered the morbid fear I experienced as an eight-years old when I lost the sight of my parents when playing in one of huge London's park playgrounds – I was abroad and totally alone - but then at least I knew that they were not dead, that I would ultimately be found and the whole thing lasted for no more than five minutes. I ensured myself that I will do everything to help this poor roe survive in the forest, I contacted the forester and volunteers and then quit the hunting club for good. Now I don't even eat meat anymore and became a volunteer at a dog shelter. My compassion flourished and I could never kill an animal again. Of course, the population of wild animals has to be controlled, but instead of taking part in that, I prefer to help these poor dogs find loving families, gathering money for their food, or driving them to a vet when they're sick and are suffering. My practice and mindfulness helped me change and I would never-ever could go back to hunting again. The second shock I had was when my friend who worked as a butcher tried to explain to me why he became a vegan. He was totally depressed with his job and wanted to quit anyway, so he invited me to the butchery- even though that was illegal – and showed me how the killing of animals really is. I don't want to preach veganism or vegetarianism in this book because it wasn't so long ago when I was in love with steaks myself, but after that visit- I really understood what the Smith's song "Meat is Murder" means. When I experienced how the animal slaughter does (including shechita) look, sound and smell – I almost fainted. You can (or maybe should) look it up on the Internet - if your stomach is strong enough. I realized how we, as humans, are extremely selfish. We put our needs over the freedom of other sentient beings, causing their extreme and unspeakable suffering, and we don't even see how it comes back to us in many ways. My life got much better when I understood that simple truth. I'm not going to convince anyone here that a Buddhist has to be a vegetarian/vegan, or that people who eat meat (all my family and almost all my friends, for that matter) are cruel, because that's not necessarily true, but you should definitely take some time to deeply reflect on that matter and then pick your own way – consciously, not blinded by any ignorance.

2. Respect other people's property – you must not steal, trespass, or otherwise covet another person's property. You must have the

courtesy to request usage of their property. There are many a time that we passively engage in acts of not respecting other people's goods. This could be as subtle as taking your friend's or family member's pen without seeking permission, or even grabbing that yoghurt in the fridge without asking your friend or spouse. Buddhism taught me never to take someone else's property without asking first. However small it is and however funny or silly it may sound, it is often these small things that we overlook that start as small ripples but spread and become big waves able to shake oceans. During my University times I took my new roommate's bread without even asking him, because I ran out of food, was hungry, it was raining, and he was still sleeping. I consumed it all... Turned out that it was gluten-free bread (I had no idea that he was diagnosed with celiac disease), and that there were no shops in neighborhood where he could buy himself a new one. More than that, he had very important exam (I was sure that he would've told me about it, but he forgot) that morning. Well – "thanks" to my lack of good manners he just had few spoons of nut butter and a glass of water, went to his exam hungry, failed, and then had to quit his summer camp as he had to write the exam again. Maybe he would have failed anyway, but you can imagine how I felt anyways, and there's a huge possibility that I was the cause of his misery. I can imagine much bigger consequences and ripple effect coming from bigger disrespect of this commandment.

3. Respect your own pure nature – To respect your own pure nature is to understand that you should be the temple of your highest good intent. Christians call it "temple of God". I am one of those

who believed that I could do anything with my body since it belonged to me. As a young man I had tattoos, some of them pretty 'offensive' and ugly. I also had dreadlocks. I could easily wear tattered clothes and I never bothered how clean they needed to be. I thought I was 'free', however, down in my heart I was a frustrated man. A man who hardly had lasting relationships and never got a lasting job. These frustrations also led me to start abusing substances. I had definitely too much Bourbon, vodka, and other perception-altering substances back then. The moment I started reading about Buddhism and practicing meditation, I learned the importance of my body as the temple of my highest good intent. I learned from Buddha that I was the creator of my own karma and thus I could change it for the better, as well as that I was the cause of my own suffering and I was the only person who had the means to end it. This was the rallying call to change my habits to start respecting my own pure, nature. I removed most of the tattoos I had (not that I have a problem with tattoos in general, but mine were really ugly, hardcore, and offensive), I completely shaved off my careless hair (dreadlocks don't suit me anyway, especially when not taken care of) and burned all those old and torn T-Shirts and shorts I had (one of the best decisions in my life, now I would prefer to wear a ballerina's leotard rather than to go out in these rags I considered 'cool'). This became my turning point. It didn't take three months before I got a proper job, started rising up the career ladder fast, and then, finally, started my own business which changed my life totally. I also went to the gym and started transforming my body (I was dangerously underweight) which improved my overall health and well-being. That, in turn, boosted my self-confidence and allowed me to meet more great people, including my wonderful girlfriend. And it all began so simply. Just the one first little step that "attracted" all the good karma.

"Do not look for a sanctuary in anyone except your self."

"To keep the body in good health is a duty...otherwise we shall not be able to keep our mind strong and clear."- Gautama Buddha

4. Respect your integrity- You should not offer false testimony against anyone, or lie for your profit. Giving lies when you are called upon as a witness, either to make someone appear as more guilty or innocent than he/she is makes you lose your integrity. Cheating on your partner or spouse also goes into this category, just like scams and not keeping promises – including those promises you have given to yourself – that's the easiest way to lose self respect, self trust, and to push yourself away from your own dreams and goals. NEVER break your promises. This is immensely practical commandment!

5. Respect your conscience – You should not corrupt your mind. Corrupting your mind may be caused by holding onto false beliefs, being addicted to intoxicating substances, or engaging in all forms of addiction, such as too much Internet, social media,

pornography, television, alcohol abuse, or watching too much violent movies, or even listening to aggressive music too often (I'm still a big rock and metal fan and I love going to concerts, but I discovered that exposing myself for this type of music everyday really makes me feel disrupted and depressed, so I also started exploring other genres or just choosing absolute silence sometimes). The end result is chaos, bad intent, bad words, and bad actions – bad karma which begets even more bad karma ad infinitum, unless and until you stop the vicious cycle.

"Teach this simple truth to all: A generous heart, kind speech, and a life of service and compassion are the things which renew humanity."- Gautama Buddha

Conclusion: Benefits of Practicing Buddhism in Everyday Life

There are many benefits of Buddhism. I summarize them into four broad categories: psychological, mental, physical, and spiritual.

The Psychological Benefits of Practicing Buddhism

Buddhism is primarily concerned with cognition, sensations, emotions, and feelings. Thus, Buddhism recognizes emotional and cognitive causes of suffering. By the enlightenment, one comes to the realization of the impermanence of suffering. The recognition that all experience is preceded by mind, made by mind, and led by mind, which brings you to the ultimate realization that you are the cause of your suffering. This bonds well with the common adage that experience and success has not so much to do with **what** really happens to you, but so much to do with **how** you respond to what happens to you.

The Mental Benefits of Practicing Buddhism

Clinical psychiatrists have alluded as to how your negative mind perceptions can lead to various mental illnesses including stress, anxiety, depression, delusion and many other serious forms of mental disorders. Practicing Buddhism purifies your mind from these wrong perceptions and thus enables you to have peace and serenity.

The Physical Benefits of Practicing Buddhism

Negative mind perceptions have been proven by many clinical psychiatrists as one of the leading causes of emotional distress. They have also shown how emotional distress can cause various physical illnesses such as ulcers, hypertension, and cardiovascular arrest. Purification of your mind through practicing Buddhism ensures that you detoxify your mind from triggering dangerous emotional affliction.

The Spiritual Benefits of Practicing Buddhism

The highest aspiration of those who seek spirituality is to be in a state of perfect harmony with the nature of one's own being, nature of other beings, and nature of things. In this state of perfect harmony, peace abounds as there are no conflicts but right knowledge and right understanding. This is the highest aspirations that those who belong to religions do seek to achieve.

Negative conflicts, violence, and wars are all attributed to ignorance and selfish desires. These selfish desires can only be conquered by compassion and wisdom, and you can only achieve an absolute compassion trough enlightenment. Thus by gaining enlightenment, one can be able to overcome all forms of illnesses, negative conflicts, violence, and wars. Right Knowledge can bring liberation to the entirety humankind and thus bring humanity to a state of perpetual joy, peace, serenity, and harmony. This state is known as Nirvana.

Gaining Enlightenment

Enlightenment is the complete and full purification of your heart from attachments, aversions, and illusions. It is letting go off your notion of independent self or independent soul. Achieving enlightenment is in essence attaining your full realization of all faculties of your human potential.

You can gain enlightenment by practicing Dharma. Dharma simply refers to the teachings of Buddha. By following the Eightfold Path, you achieve right knowledge and right liberation. Right knowledge is seeing things as they truly are and not as they appear to be nor as sages want them to be. The fruit of right knowledge is right liberation.

Entering Nirvana

Entering nirvana is the ultimate state that those who practice Dharma accomplish after achieving enlightenment – but trust me - even the consciousness alone of getting closer and closer to enlightenment and just being a better person will make you **much happier!**

Endgame

Nothing is eternal in this world, and so the times has come for me to finish this book. I'd like to thank you again for choosing it! I hope that you have grasped the pure essence of Buddhism and that this work will help you in your journey towards being a better person.

In fact, Buddhism can be summarized in just few words: morality, compassion, mental concentration, and wisdom. These four are able to make your life strikingly better.

If you think that Buddhism is for you and you're hungry for more, I'd like to recommend you these few titles as a further lecture and a follow-up:

- First of all, it is a great idea to study **Dhammapa**, which is a collection of Buddha's sayings. You should be able to find it in libraries, on the Internet, or to simply buy it. It's a way to understand Buddha's teachings and also a great source of everyday inspiration and wisdom.

- I encourage you to read everything on **Pāli Canon** of Buddhism (also known as "**Tipitaka**"). It is one of the most complete early canons in Buddhism. Here's an interesting library from which you can start:

  http://www.accesstoinsight.org/lib/index.html

- Here you can also find some great Buddhist stories! Just follow the link and there you go: http://www.buddhanet.net/bt1_conts.htm

  Mind you that most of them are symbolical, but they show the Buddhist morality and "how the things are".

- Another interesting and important positions would be **Jataka Tales** – the story about former lives of Buddha (you should also mind that they are symbolical, and fable-like – I threat them more like an example of Buddhist art) and **Visuddhimagga** ("The Path of Purification") – which is a very practical guide and definitely a "must read" for every aspiring Buddhist.

- Ok, enough reading for now! Let's watch a movie! South Korean **"Spring, Summer, Fall, Winter... and Spring"** from 2003 directed by Ki-duk Kim. A great allegory of life, karma, and human existence in general. Along with the young Buddhist monk you will be experiencing the story of his life from spring through winter. A very different picture if you're used to American Hollywood productions – this one is really silent and calm - I really enjoyed it. And about the last scene (no, it's not really a spoiler) – yes, that's possible in real life at the highest levels of mastery. That's what meditation does to you.

- Why won't you also try listening to some Tibetan Mantras? I just love how they relax me and help me in my meditations:

http://y2u.be/2kIfq4nra2Q

More than that, a good idea might be to look for a local Buddhist community. I live in a relatively small town (about 180.000 people) but there are a few communities, so I'm sure that you will be able to find something for you as well. I met lots of great people - friends for life – and found many interesting things about myself. It was definitely worth it. A community made of worthy people will also help you incorporate these teachings into your life and stick to them.

Lastly, please take a moment to think what can you change in your life **right now?**

Not tomorrow, not next year – but **now**. Just think of one little step and make it now. Should it be meditation? Or maybe reconciliation with someone who used to be close to you? A deep reflection on your emotions?

It's **your choice now.**

Finally, if you enjoyed this book, I would really appreciate your honest review on Amazon! That would definitely be a good karma!

Keep well and **may you have a happy and fulfilling life!**

"However many holy words you read, however many you speak,
what good will they do you if you do not act on upon them?" -
Guatama Buddha

Recommended Reading for You:

If you are interested in Self-Development, NLP, Psychology, Social Dynamics, PR, Soft Skills and related topics, you might be interested in previewing or downloading my other books:

-> Meditation for Beginners: How to Meditate (As an Ordinary Person!) to Relieve Stress and be Successful

Meditation is not about crystals, hypnotic folk music and incense sticks!
Forget about sitting in unnatural and uncomfortable positions while going "ommmmm...."
It is not a club full of yoga masters, Shaolin monks, hippies and new-agers.
It is super practical and universal practice which can improve your overall brain performance and happiness.
When meditating, you take a step back from actively thinking your thoughts, and instead, see them for what they are. The reason why meditation is helpful in reducing stress and attaining peace is that it gives your over-active conscious a break.
Just like your body needs it, your mind does too!
I give you the gift of peace that I was able to attain through present moment awareness.

Direct link: http://www.amazon.com/dp/B00KQRU9BC/

You may also want to buy the paperback version of "Meditation for Beginners":

http://goo.gl/USTj4n

-> Gain Self-Confidence Fast With NLP

In this you'll read about the **most effective NLP tools in the context of permanent self-esteem boost**, but also my mindset, the right approach that actually works and I'll share a few personal stories that will motivate you. I'll tell you how to stick to your personal change plan and how to start a journey towards being a better person!

Direct link: http://www.amazon.com/dp/B00IEJSJoC/

->Improve Your Relationship Fast with NLP

All interpersonal conflicts have three key ingredients; **wrong perceptions, improper communication and destructive behavioral patterns.** NLP gives us simple and yet effective techniques to **redirect those perceptions, significantly enhance communication** with the people we care about and **reprogram those negative behavioral patterns** forever so that our relationships can flourish! In this book not only I'll show you the **most effective NLP tools in the context of permanent relationship improvement**, but also my mindset, the right approach that actually works in relationships and I'll tell you **how to enhance your communication skills** and how to start a journey towards being a better partner and family member!

Direct Link: http://www.amazon.com/dp/B00J7oHWYG/

->Stress Management with NLP

I was always stressed to the max. When I was young, **I was called a worry-wart and told that I would have a heart-attack, ulcer or be bald by the age of 16.**

At some point of my life I came to the conclusion that my nervousness got way too dangerous and **I HAD** to find a solution and **finally calm down**. I would read books, watch DVD's, talk to people and go to seminars. And then – finally - I found the answer. **In this book I'll show you NLP tools tailor-made for stress and anxiety management** and my favorite **relaxation techniques that helped me.** You will also read how to **minimize stressors and adverse circumstances** that keep you **anxious and nervous** and about the **right mindset and lifestyle you should have to maintain low stress level, finally relax and stop worrying...**

Direct link: http://www.amazon.com/dp/B00JGVZ8L0/

-> Speed Reading: How to Read 3-5 Times Faster and Become an Effective Learner

No matter if your objective is to **do great during your University exams**, become a **bestselling writer**, or start **your own**

business, you will have to read A LOT, and I mean it. Reading takes time. **Time is our most valuable asset** - nothing new here.

You can always make money or meet new friends, but **you will never be able to "make time".** The only way to succeed and have a happy life without regrets is to use it wisely and **learn how to manage and save it.**

In this book, I will take you through the dynamics of speed reading in a way you may have never imagined before. I'm here to preach the need for speed reading and make use of some of the principles that can steer your knowledge and productivity in the right direction.

Learn How To Read 5 Times Faster, Remember Much More and Save Massive Time!

In This Book You Will Read About:

-The History Of Speed Reading
-Popular Speed Reading Myths
-**Environment and Preparation**
-How To Measure Your Reading Speed
-**Key Speed Reading Techniques**
-Reading Tips for Computer and Tablet
-Common Reading Mistakes to Avoid
-Easy and Effective Memory/Learning Techniques
-**Dealing with Tests and Diagrams**
-**Practical Exercises and Eye Adjustments**
-Useful Links and Ideas
-Diet
-How to Track Your Progress
-Proper Motivation and Mindset

Direct Buy Link: http://www.amazon.com/dp/B00NLVIP2O/

Paperback version: http://goo.gl/WsvDfm

->Zen: Beginner's Guide: Happy, Peaceful and Focused Lifestyle for Everyone

Contrary to popular belief, Zen is not a discipline reserved for monks practicing Kung Fu. Although there is some truth to this idea, Zen is a practice that is applicable, useful, and pragmatic for anyone to study regardless of what religion you follow (or don't follow).

Zen is the practice of studying your subconscious and **seeing your true nature.**

The purpose of this work is to show you how to apply and utilize the teachings and essence of Zen in everyday life in the Western society. I'm not really an "absolute truth seeker" unworldly type of person - I just believe in practical plans and blueprints that actually help in living a better life. Of course I will tell you about the origin of Zen and the traditional ways of practicing it, but I will also show you my side of things, my personal point of view and translation of many Zen truths through a more "contemporary" and practical language.

It is a "modern Zen lifestyle" type of book.

What You Will Read About:

• Where Did Zen Come From? - A short history and explanation of Zen
• What Does Zen Teach? - The major teachings and precepts of Zen
• Various Zen meditation techniques that are applicable and practical for everyone!
• The benefits of a Zen lifestyle
• What Zen Buddhism is NOT?

- How to slow down and start enjoying your life
- How to accept everything and lose nothing
- Why being alone can be beneficial
- Why pleasure is NOT happiness
- Six Ways to Practically Let Go
- How to de-clutter your life and live simply
- "Mindfulness on Steroids"
- How to Take Care of your Awareness and Focus
- Where to start and how to practice Zen as a regular person
- And many other interesting concepts...

I invite you to take this journey into the peaceful world of Zen Buddhism with me today!

Direct Buy Link: http://www.amazon.com/dp/B00PWUBSEK

Paperback version: http://goo.gl/dxtu9d

You may also want to buy Kindle version of this book:

Buddhism: Beginner's Guide:

http://goo.gl/wJqjyX

@

My Mailing list: If you would like to receive fresh info about **new Kindle reads** on social dynamics, psychology, career, NLP, success and healthy living for **free** <u>I invite you to my Mailing List.</u> Whenever my new book is out, I set the promotional price/free period for two days. You will get an e-mail notification and will **be the first to get the book free** during its limited promotion.

Why would I do this when it took me countless hours to write these e-books? First of all, that's my way of saying **"thank you"** to my new readers. Second of all – **I want to spread the word about my books and ideas.** Mind you that I hate spam and e-mails that come too frequently - no worries about that.

If you think that's a good idea and are in, just follow the link:

http://eepurl.com/R_UhP

Also, follow me on Twitter: https://twitter.com/IanTuhovsky

Would you like to be the first one to find out about free and bargain eBooks for your mental, physical and emotional wellbeing as well as personal success?

Simply follow us on Facebook:

www.facebook.com/HolisticWellnessBooks

We have created this page with a few fellow authors of mine. We hope you find it inspiring and helpful.

Thank You for your time and interest in our work!

Ian & Holistic Wellness eBooks

About The Author

Ian is an avid reader and writer and he calls himself "the observer of people and reality". He had always been interested in studying the human mind and the society. Ian holds a BA degree in Sociology and apart from writing and investigation he works as a HR consultant for many European companies from various sectors.

In his free time he really enjoys travelling and getting to know different cultures. His favorite way of travelling is a spontaneous, adventurous travelling on a very little budget- something he has been doing since he was a teenager and became a part of his lifestyle. Hitchhiking, as well as using services like "couch surfing" are his preferred modes of immersing himself into new cultures and staying out of his comfort zone. He just loves the thrill of unpredictable travelling!

Another passion of Ian's is music. He plays the guitar, sings and composes music. He is also an electronic music producer- something he does as a hobby. As a child and a teenager, Ian suffered from shyness and low self-esteem. Looking for solutions he would find consolation in doing lots of reading and writing songs. It wasn't until he began to confront his fears and do exactly the opposite that his brain was telling him. He likes putting his experiences on paper, who knows maybe they can inspire you in a way?

Made in the USA
San Bernardino, CA
04 February 2015